My Sapphire:

My Journey

To

My Purpose

CASSANDRA WHITE

Manufactured in the United States of America

ISBN-13: 979-8-9857140-6-7

FIRST EDITION –

Editors: Tuesday White & WesCourt Advisors

USA $14.99

DEDICATION

This book is dedicated to my mother, my late Grandma Pinkie, and to all the amazing women of God who motivated and inspired me. They taught me to never give up on my dream, always keep God first in my life, and to love with my pure heart. I want to bless and thank all of you for reading my book and going on this journey with me.

Acknowledgments

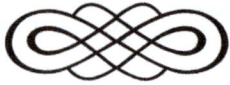

Thank you to everyone who supported me along this journey. Special thanks to my editor, Tuesday White (White Standard Press), and my publisher, Dr. Adair, for helping make this dream a reality.

Table of Contents

PART I

Faith, Family, and Love

"Now faith is the substance of things hoped for, the evidence of things not seen."

Hebrews 11:1 KJV

What is faith?

A faithful life is no 100-meter dash; it is more like a 5K marathon. The kind of faith described in The Bible as 'saving faith" is ongoing and requires daily maintenance. We see it around us every day. We see it at work throughout the seasons of our lives when we can look back and realize that the hard times do not last forever. A faithful life is like an Olympic Marathon; it requires strength and endurance. "Saving faith," in the Bible, is described as ongoing and requires nurturing and consistency.

It is more than just a few prayers here and there. It is more than just setting fanciful goals and projections. It is cultivating willpower and channelling inner strength. It is about putting into action the good intentions in our hearts.

It must permeate throughout your entire existence.

My faith has always been my lifetime guarantee that I would find my true purpose when the timing of life allowed it. Faith has been my guarantee throughout my life that I would find my true purpose when the time was right.

I am thankful to have been guided by my faith on this journey. My Big Mama, Nana, and Grandma have inspired me along the way. I can remember leaning solely on the understanding that having a kind and caring heart would lead me to my passion. I was taught to trust that God had a great plan for my life. I was encouraged to lean on my faith to overcome my problems.

Young, Faithful Love

From my understanding, as a young woman, I was convinced that loving myself and trusting God ultimately was fundamental to attracting the kind of love I wanted from a partner. I imagined love to be all-encompassing, and the man who was right for me would love me that way. I was taught that a woman's faith in God makes her confident. She knows that her sacrifices are based on God's divine plan for her life. Every sacrifice is a part of God's grand scheme for her. When it comes to love and marriage, the sacrifice is no different. We know what God wants from us when it comes to starting a family and aligning with the right person for us. Even if we try to run from our understanding, we know deep down inside that when love is authentic, that sacrifice will happen despite the significant changes it brings to our lives.

This makes one wonder why, around the world, the word *love* is used very casually. We say that we love sports, success, and the smell of the sea breeze. Further, most dictionaries define love as a feeling of strong or constant affection for a person; an attraction that includes sexual desire; a person you love in a romantic way.

Yet, the true essence of love, the love that leads to marriage, is something else.

That kind of love is not just a noun; it is a verb; it's what you *do* that is true love. You will shift, you will change, and you will grow.

I've always known that love, at first sight, was not impossible, but it rarely happens. Pulling now from my memories, my first encounter with love may not have been at first sight, but when it came at me, it came quickly.

It happened on a hot summer's day while walking in a beautiful garden. I ended up running into the young man that I had a crush on. He was tall and handsome, and he seemed to say all the right things to me. My cheeks would flush red when he called me *Niecy*. When he called me beautiful, there was no denying that I was smitten.

Still, there was more to it. What he showed me was something different; it was the love I had wondered about. It was *real* love that came from the inside and spilled out onto me. The love found me because I chose to trust God to help me on my journey to loving myself and discovering what was for me.

I was young, but I understood what God wanted for me in a husband. We would not always be able to finish each other's sentences or know each other's thoughts. But, when it came to the fundamentals and foundation of life, we would know how you felt about having children, how we would raise them, and where we wanted to live. I understand that true love was more than just "falling in love'" it was about growing in love. The only way we would truly know each other would be to invest in the time to do so. Marriage would seal the deal on our pursuit of love and happiness. With all the butterflies and rainbows, we both understood that real love meant good and bad times, times of good health and times of sickness, times of enduring patience, and times of outbursts of anger. All of those things flashed before our eyes that day in the garden. And still, this man looked me in the eyes and said that he would make me happy if I trusted him.

So, I did. We started dating, and my world changed. We took many long walks together, sharing many secrets over time. When I was with him, I could imagine nothing but our life together. I introduced him to my family, and they loved him. When he told me he was enlisting in the Air Force, I begged him not to leave me. He assured me that he was putting things in motion to enable me to join him when the time was right. Of course, my joining him would mean we would have to marry. And, he would have to ask my father's permission.

Permission was granted, and with my father's blessing and God's grace, our journey.

On May 11, 1985, we were married. Earlier, we found out that I was pregnant and set a date for the wedding shortly after completing his basic training. A few days after, he left for London, where he would be stationed. I would be able to join him a few months later in that September.

Although the next few months were stressful with us being separated, nothing made me happier than being a wife and mother. All the plans for a life full of love and adventure had me excited. My husband was true to his word and his promise to make me happy. To be loved by him felt right, and so did everything else that happened shortly after.

A World Apart

I was 21, still a girl, yet soon a mother when I arrived in London. The culture shock took me back. I was from Griffin, in Spalding County, Georgia, and this was a world apart. My first son was born two weeks after I arrived, and the reality hit hard. I was married, in a foreign country, and very emotional. It was overwhelming, to say the least, and I needed to figure out how to navigate this new life better sooner than later.

This was an interval in life where the teachings of faith instilled in me needed to take charge. And they did.

I met April shortly after we were settled in London. She was a great help to me when adjusting to this new life. She taught me the basics for navigating the life of an army wife. I learned how to calculate a currency I was unfamiliar with from her. She guided me when it came to doing household shopping for food and necessities. She even tutored me on the basics of London culture.

April seamlessly became a close friend and occasional babysitter. Without a doubt, she was a Godsend. She had a kind, gentle demeanor that made everything seem easier. As I think about her now, this was the point in my life where I realized how much I was thankful that God made each of us special and unique. We are made in grace and show love and kindness differently. The timing of April's place in my life was indeed divine alignment.

Things started to fall into line. My role as a housewife was taking on its shape and form. My husband and I were getting to know each other more and more along the way. We were getting to know ourselves as parents. I treasured the time we spent together in those early years.

Despite the upside of things, he was still gone a lot. There were downtimes. I had the baby keep my company, but my longing for his company would take its toll as time passed. Married life was not as easy as I supposed it would be. There was a need for more than just love, and on this part of my journey, that realization was hitting me hard.

I did my best to stay focused on being the best wife and mother that I could be, and on reinforcing this, I held steadfast to and developed my faith in God. This faith would give me the strength needed to endure the ups and downs. I was blessed to be a wife and mother. I was loved and protected. I had stability.

And still, something was missing.

In time, I started making friends. They were older and married, so I was able to lean on them for guidance and advice. We went out and enjoyed the sites around London. There were Cathedrals and Castles; everything was grand and beautiful. The bustling city from the double-deckers buses was exciting to behold. I was learning things, and it was all changing me. I was becoming the woman God had intended me to be. I felt, for a time, that I was grasping the more profound meaning.

Although I was forming stronger bonds, I became aware that sometimes, people did not think and feel the way I did. I had to learn to appreciate these friendships for what they were and accept that not everyone was as enthralled about understanding me as I was.

I went on in my role as a dedicated wife and mother as my husband stayed busy working and taking care of us. I did my best to care for my sons and all the household responsibilities that were mine.

I was so young, and there were times when it was difficult making others happy while trying to find myself. I fell into a state of depression sometimes, and it was there that I prayed more and more to God.

This marriage was God's union, which was now the beginning of one of its stormy seasons. I was navigating things as best as I could. I was leveraging the power of prayer when making decisions and always looking toward brighter days.

I had to face facts. The ugly truth is that marriage going through ugly is very normal. All marriages see different seasons. Some seasons are blissful and exciting. Others seasons are sullen, stressful, and lack passion. But, just imagine that the hard times are when God is doing his most profound work on our hearts.

Whether we admit it or not, we are all self-involved within our marriages. We do not consistently think of ourselves as a union. We absolutely do hang on to some of our individuality. We have our own views, needs, and wants. We can't really help that.

But, at the end of the day, we must be willing to serve and sacrifice in the marriage. But, faithfulness leads us back to God and helps us to seek humility and better understand the way He is working on us.

This is how I had to work through the hard times with my husband.

God uses hard times in marriage to reveal selfishness in my life

and unrealistic expectations. When things in a marriage become challenging, as a result, we can see God's hand redirecting our attention to Him. It's hard to know how to work on your marriage when you're not on the same page, but submitting to God and having candid but hard conversations is an excellent place to start.

I was learning, at this young age, that bad times come and go.

In this new life, I found myself coming to understand how men and women were so different, yet very much alike, in a faraway city. As a wife, I was meant to be a part of my husband, as the Bible clearly teaches the woman came from the rib of man. Yet, the pressing issue of my own identity was very much forefront in my mind.

Motherhood

My son was growing into a young boy fast. I was determined to teach my son to always love and respect women. I wanted him to grow up knowing that a good woman is also God-fearing and family-oriented. I had to be his example as he was growing up so quickly, absorbing everything around him. Some of my biggest inspirations came from my family. Big mama, Nana, and grandma truly inspired me by their stories and experiences. I saw how vital Faith and God were to them. I was his family, and I would teach him well.

Two years after coming to London, I was pregnant again. I leaned even more heavily on my faith as my family grew. Motherhood had changed me and was still changing me. But my motives were pure. The hearts of my husband and children were safely entrusted to me. I was blessed to be a mother – it was a part of my calling to teach, lead, love, and serve them. It would not be easy, but it was my fate, and in these early days, God did some of his best work on my character.

PART II

Faith & Purpose

California

I was still pregnant as we transitioned to my husband's second post in California. We were now in the land of big dreams, money, and fame. Almost right away, I took in how the people in this new town loved to party. I would jokingly say I could become a movie star and make a ton of money; maybe that would help my problems go away.

Deep down, I knew that God had a different plan for me. So, I always wanted to know Him and develop a relationship with Him. I continued to seek His guidance in prayer, asking Him to help me with self-love. I also prayed about finding a way to help others. So many times, even when I needed help and prayer for myself, I found myself praying for others when I needed someone to pray for me.

I read my Bible, and I knew that if we do not live to seek God, it can only be because we do not really believe Him or that He is not worthy of our attention. To continuously pursue Him would be of utmost importance to my faith. My commitment could never diminish if I were to find my way in the world. Despite my challenges, I wanted to always be intentional and persistent about moving towards God. It was *hard*, but I could *not* become stagnant.

Around this time, in California, I began to dwell constantly on my discontentment. My soul wasn't at peace. I didn't understand why the people around me didn't easily befriend me. A part of me was lonely, and a part of me was holding on by threads to my faith. I even tried buying their friendship, but it was all to no avail. They still hurt me. You would think I would learn my lesson quickly and give up on pleasing people so they can like me.

I had to pray my way out of that mindset. The more I prayed and began my relationship with God, the more I learned what God would mean to my life. My goal was to always find my purpose on this earth. I knew I was passionate about empowering and motivating people to get closer to God.

Faith in Finding My Purpose

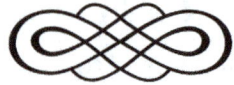

Soon after arriving in California, my second son was born. I had prayed for a daughter, but God had found it fitting to bless me with another son, and so, I was grateful all the same.

Living in California, it was easy to see how influencing the fast and glamourous city could be. For a very brief time, I *did* think I might become a movie and make a ton of money. Maybe that would satisfy the longing I had to find my purpose. In the end, I couldn't see myself gaining so much materialistically and still not having a peaceful heart.

I simply did not fit in with the crowd around me, and I had to find out why. It was not so I could change my life to blend. Instead, I sought to come into my purpose.

I leaned again on my faith and how I was brought up to pray and trust in God. I would find my way, I was sure. I would continue to seek his guidance and develop a solid and unbreakable bond. I wanted to be constant with my self-love and share kindness and care for others.

My requests for just how I would do this were not clear to me yet. But I remained as positive as I could. There were times I felt lost in it all, and I needed others to pray for me the way I did them. I needed reassurance. Yet, for the most part, I was alone. I had to learn to pray for and by myself. I had to make it enough.

I learned in this season that often, God does not answer our prayers immediately. Sometimes things get worse before they get better. It will seem as though our timeline doesn't align with God's timetable. This is where the weight, width, and depth of our faith come into question.

There's a scripture for this in the Bible. It was about the Canaanite woman[1]. Her faith was so strong, and she profoundly and wholly believed that any salvation that came to her daughter would come directly from Christ. And it did. I needed to affirm my faith this way. I was confident it would lead me to clarity when it came to pinpointing my purpose.

---

[1] Matthew 15: 21-28

As I continued to pray in my faith, my passion for others and childcare began to grow. I discovered that I loved working with small children and seeing them develop and grow into productive adults.

Another World Apart

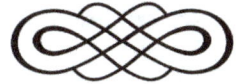

As my boys were growing up, my husband and I were growing apart. Between trying to find myself and raise up my boys, my marriage was falling apart. No, I didn't want to separate. I still loved him so much. Why?

Was it because we were not ready for marriage? I didn't understand how love could come and go. Did I not make him happy anymore?

I became increasingly vulnerable and self-conscious. I prayed to Jesus to keep my marriage together, but it seemed like the prayers were not working.

Living as a woman of faith requires us to be all in, fully convinced that God is who He says He is, has done what He said He would do and will continue to be faithful to His word. Perfection may be impossible; being a woman of faith is not. We tend to make faith more complicated than it needs to be. And it was at this point in my life, I had to go back to the foundation of faith. I had to refresh, renew, and relearn.

What exactly was my faith? What was it made up of?

We know that faith is something that is required of us. We cannot do the work of pleasing God without it. It is vital. Knowing that should drive us to search out what faith actually is. We hear the word quite often in Christian circles, but, in a candid moment, can we stand with a firm grasp on understanding it? I needed so badly to grasp this understanding.

Eventually, my husband came to me and said that he was leaving. I pleaded with him not to and tried to work things out. But he said that he had to go. This was the most challenging thing to ever happen to me. All I could remember was to try my best to hold myself together for my boys. I began to think that I couldn't raise my two boys on my own. I cried and told myself I couldn't do it without him. I had never been on my own having to do it all.

Going through the divorce was tough because he was my life; our family was my life. Being from a small town and having a big wedding, I was worried about what people would say. I had to face my fear and deal with it head-on because I had two wonderful sons to stay strong for. I went to Church and put everything on the Altar.

I asked for God's help because I had done things my way, but now it was time to do the right thing for not only my boys but for me, Cassandra. I was upset because we were married ten plus years, but I felt like I didn't know him at all.

In time, if felt God spoke to my heart. I felt him say, "I'm with you through this." I started to pull my faith forefront. My life was turning a corner. Things were shifting and changing once again. My marriage was over, yes. But something else growing within me.

The Bible says, "But without faith, it is impossible to please Him: for he that cometh to God must believe that He is and that He is a rewarder of them that diligently seek him." [2]

Living a purposeful life comes down to this very verse.

---

[2] Hebrews 11:6

The Substance
of Things Hoped For

After the divorce, I began working in the childcare field. I quickly started to grow in my passion and purpose. God began to tell me that I was on the right path and there would be no distractions.

As this part of the journey began, my faith blossomed immensely. It was true: when God is in it, things will work out for your good[3]. As time went on, I began to feel better and gain my own independence.

With this newfound independence, my boys would often tell me that we would be okay. Their love and affection helped me see how fortunate and blessed I was as their mother.

---

[3] Romans 8:28

Time went on, and life started to get easier for my boys and me. Although we were divorced, I kept a positive relationship with their father, so my boys could see that it didn't matter if we were not together. We could co-parent effectively because it was important for them to have their father in their lives.

On this new path, I met women that were on similar paths as I was. Some were different circumstances, some good, some bad, but we were all on the same journey in the end. On the uncertain journey, we were all comfortable with a specific way of living our lives. Now everything was different, and we had to start a new chapter of life on the fly.

My life began to take shape, definitely somewhat different than what I was used to. On weekends the boys went with their father, and I began going to Church consistently. I also began to go out and experience this new life path I was embarking on. Although I was out and about, I was uncomfortable enough to bring a man around my boys. My hope was that it would happen naturally on God's time, rather than forcing it.

Everything was working for my good, it seemed. I knew it was my trust in God. I just knew that despite the times my faith may have wavered, I always came back to it, stronger than before.

The Bible says, "Trust in the Lord with all your heart and do not lean on your own understanding. In all your ways, acknowledge him, and he will make straight your paths."[4]

And this is what I did.

But it was not enough to know what my life's purpose was. I needed to do something about it. To fulfill this purpose, I needed to pursue this purpose every single day. My actions needed to be intentional.

I realized that the trials and tests must come before the rewards. The walk of a woman of faith may be challenging, but it is worth it. Even when I felt I lost so much when my marriage ended, I didn't lose sight of the fact that my faith assured that my story wasn't over.

My passion for children had become clear. I also wanted to be a light for older adults and show them how bright they could shine with God in their lives. I remember my mom, grandmother, and aunties demonstrating strength and faith. Each of them was a positive woman, even with the ups and downs of life. They taught my sister and me that disappointment will come in life, but how you approach the ups and downs is what matters most. I understood that some of the pain I experienced was my fault because I did not communicate what I was genuinely feeling at times. I was still trying to love those who were not lovable, but I didn't let that deter me from giving my best to people.

---

[4] Proverbs 3:5-6

Love and compassion for my family and others, I believe is a gift from above.

Not everyone will understand your mission or purpose. They don't share your vision. You cannot allow their negative opinions to stop you from moving forward.

Self-actualization begins with purposeful living. Finding your purpose and aligning with the focus and desire needed to be successful is what matters.

A lot of people around us feeling inside that they aren't smart enough to be successful at what they truly want to pursue. Their way of thinking makes them undermine their abilities and greatness. It is so important to understand that it is not how smart you are and how much you know. It is about how you use it.

Moving beyond your shortcomings and limitations to pursue your purpose requires you put aside the opinions of others.

Even More Faith

A s time went on, my boys were growing up fast. God made way for me to provide them, and I was very thankful.

Although I was out and about, I was uncomfortable enough to bring a man around my boys. My hope was that it would happen naturally on God's time, rather than forcing it.

I remember starting to feel lonely and a little sad. I wanted companionship. My life was on track, and with my heart in a better place, I knew that I would be ready to date if I met the right person.

I met a guy through a mutual friend. He was always nice and said sweet things to me. Subconsciously, I told myself he was full of lies like most men were. But as time passed, he convinced me to go out on a date every Wednesday night.

When my sons asked, *"Mommy, are you seeing somebody?"* I quickly replied, telling them to stay out of *grown folks' business*. My oldest son then said, *"Yes, she is,"* to his little brother.

They asked if they could meet my new friend, and I told them not quite yet.

This was very new to me, so I felt like I couldn't bring him around until things were serious between us because my boys were and still is everything to me. So time went on, and things began to get serious. We decided to tell his three girls and my two boys.

I was both nervous and excited about this new love. I wondered if my boys would accept and like him. I wondered if his girls would accept and like my boys and me. He met my boys, and I met his girls, and everything went well. I was so excited because I had always wanted a baby girl, and now I had three!

As time moved on, we decided to move in together. I didn't want to be married again for a while, but I also didn't want to be single, so I had a major decision to make. I was a little confused while trying to find love and trust a man again wholeheartedly. I realized that we just had to take our time. I never wanted to be taken for granted again. I was a woman on a new journey, so I wanted this new man to accept me for me. I wanted him to value and appreciate a real woman who was on a journey to find her way in this life. My ultimate goal was to start a home that put

God first and family second. This was my new journey to find my purpose.

On this journey, I am now at the crossroad where my dreams and desires meet with my faith and purpose.

I used to dream about having a daughter of my own, but God gave me two sons instead. Now, I had the opportunity to motivate and empower three girls who came into my life.

I may be a world away from the 21-year-old girl lost in London, but I am so much closer to God and currently living my best life. I will always treasure the learning experiences and the hard times that have made me stronger.

I am often reminded that God takes His time with us. Over time, He molds and refines us. He loves us too much to let us go through challenges without teachable moments. Our wisdom and understanding, faithfulness, and good character are gently given to us through our trust in Him. I make it a point to always remember that what God is doing in the seasons when it seems we are just waiting is simply helping us to embrace the refining in our lives.

Here is one last scripture that helps us to understand that all things are possible with enduring faith,

32 Remember those earlier days after you had received the light when you endured in a great conflict full of suffering. 33 Sometimes you were publicly exposed to insult and persecution; at other times, you stood side by side with those who were so treated. 34 You suffered along with those in prison and joyfully accepted the confiscation of your property because you knew that you yourselves had better and lasting possessions. 35 So do not throw away your confidence; it will be richly rewarded. – Hebrews 10: 32-35

www.ingramcontent.com/pod-product-compliance
Lightning Source LLC
Chambersburg PA
CBHW060358130626
46553CB00003B/1285